# I KNOW A PLACE

## A COLLECTION OF POEMS
## BY PETER DONNDELINGER

# Table of Contents

Acknowledgements                                      1

Remembering Margee                                    3

Living                                                5

    Elusive Beauty                6

    Righting Wrongs               7

    Consoling Moon                8

    Day in A-Minor                9

    Another First Hello           10

    A Meandering Brook            12

    Adirondack Chairs             13

    Wisdom                        14

    Awakening                     15

    Encounter with My Dad in the Grocery Store    16

    What You Do Not Own           18

    Traffic Light                 19

    Embrace Solitude              20

    Cloud                         21

Longing                                               23

    Butterfly                     24

    Table for Two                 25

    The Garden                    26

The Button 27

Embers 28

After the Rain 29

At the Feeder 30

Lonely Days 31

Last Laundry 32

Of Course She Did 33

Table for Two - II 34

Space Walk 35

Stripped Away 36

I Go to Water 37

Reflecting 39

The Aging Face in the Mirror 40

Reflections 41

Naked 42

The Visitor 43

Dark Matter 44

Morning Walk in the Country 45

Walk a Paved Path 46

Sun Rose in the Eastern Sky 47

Conversations with Crescent Moon 48

Conversations with Crescent Moon - II 49

Somewhere                                      50

The Painted Corner                             51

She Boards the Last Train Out of Town          52

Intersection                                   53

At the Freeway Entrance                        54

Push, Pull                                     56

The Mirror                                     57

A Soft Snow                                    58

Moon                                           59

The Climb                                      60

Emerging                                       61

The Owl and the Lark                           62

The Perseids                                   63

She Danced on White Sand Dunes                 64

Painting with Oils                             65

Star Fall                                      66

Moonlit Snow                                   67

I Step Toward You                              68

It's Okay                                      69

Honey Bee                                      70

The Cotton Mask                                71

Split Personality                             72

Sky as Clear as Sky Can Be                    73

Triangulation                                 74

She Swam in Moonglade                         75

I Know a Place                                76

About the Author                              78

# Acknowledgements

I wish to thank all who supported me through the journey of writing this book.

I am grateful to my friends in the La Crosse Area Writer's Group. Their constant support and gentle prodding has made me a better writer. I thank Terri Karsten, who first published my words. I give a special shout-out to our Fireside Poetry group, including Kelly, Michelle, and Bill, who always leave me laughing and thinking about new prompts.

I owe a huge debt of gratitude to my friends Nicki, Maureen, and Paul, who have spent endless hours reading, and re-reading my poetry. Without their thoughtful edits, this collection would never have come to fruition.

I thank the Wisconsin Fellowship of Poets, publishers of *Bramble Literary Magazine* (Summer 2020) for publishing *Butterfly*. And again, a thank you to Terri Karsten at Wagonbridge Publishing for including *Last Laundry* in her anthology, *Lost and Found: Tales of Things Gone Missing.*

To my family, I owe a huge thank you. Their support has been unconditional.

Finally, thank you, Karrie, for listening to my poems.

Remembering Margee

# Living

**Elusive Beauty**

Ineffective words spill on a page
like errant paint spatters a canvas.
A frustrating struggle in persistence
to find depth from nothing.
Word replaces word. Analogy alters metaphor.
Start over. Keep everything.
Change the pallet? A fresh page.
Block in? Set the scene.
A fresh brush? A raw line.
An untried color? A new meaning.
A clean edge? A polished phrase.
Blend? Emend.
Stop. Step away.
Give it space to breathe.
To grow. To stumble. To walk.
To run in sunshine, to play in moonlight.
The piece directs the path.
Do as it says. Not as you will.
Finality is an apparition.
Elusive. Shimmering. Evanescent.

**Righting Wrongs**

Even the sunset cannot
undo all the damage
the wind has caused
by spreading its lies
about the clouds.

Only the sanguine hand
of dawn can draw
forth a sunrise.

**Consoling Moon**

I saw you wink,
as a shooting star split the night.
And caught your grin,
when I reached to cup you in my palm.

You are a playful moon this eve,
my melancholy thoughts perceive.

I am not a naive beholder,
and sense your hand upon my shoulder,
guiding me on the way,
to the dawn of a sunlit day.

**Day in A-Minor**

Melancholy mind,
beckons contemplative thoughts.
Tranquil chord dissolves.

## Another First Hello

I enter your small room,
meet your vacant gaze,
and reintroduce myself
for what must be the
hundredth time.

You speak about how rude
your neighbor was to
you this morning.
A neighbor I know you
haven't seen in over
forty years.

You tell me how much
you love your cat.
A cat I know you've
never had.

Your eyes brighten in
recognition as you ask
about my son
by name.

Does he like living
in the big city? Is his
wife happy in their
new life? How are his
kids adjusting to
their new school?
A bird —

landing on a branch
outside your window
catches your attention.
You look back at me
with eyes as empty as
Nebraska.

I reintroduce
myself for the
hundred-and-first time.

## A Meandering Brook

Her mind is a swirl of eddies
and currents, slowly moving
in untold directions.
Along shadowed shorelines
of her forgotten past,
ferns stretch skyward beside
lavender blossoms of columbine.
The stream narrows, and narrows,
and narrows, as she drifts
quietly to the sea.

**Adirondack Chairs**

The aging pair
sit side by side
near the base of wooden deck.

Armrests touch
as holding hands
affirming strength of yoke.

Weathered, cracked, strained,
holding strong.
Passed through families.
Survivors steady, present, true,
ready for shared conversations
or loving laughs.

Inseparable through time,
aging in daily sameness
amidst nature's comfortable silence,
they await sunset.

## Wisdom

It cannot be hurried
or manufactured.
It builds on bedrock
of ancient knowledge.
Slowly. Steadily. Surely.
It is ever-changing,
like the light of a star,
just arriving in the now,
after traveling an infinite
path through space and time.

### Awakening

A new revolution,
for new revelations,
of new affirmations,
with new confirmations,
of self.

**Encounter with My Dad in the Grocery Store**

You were in the soup aisle
pondering cans of chicken noodle soup.
In your cart a box of saltines
rested beside a bundle of asparagus.
Mom loved asparagus.
We made eye contact
and I saw myself reflected in
your face, graying hair, and thinning combover.
Your calm expression was the same
as it appeared on the day you retired.
The day we now know that
you'd beaten back stresses of war,
and the post-traumatic demons holding you captive.

Seeing you reminded me of my youth.
Winding the mantle clock. Baiting a hook.
Nightly dinners with you and Mom.
Adolescent struggles to separate.
Ignored opportunities to reconcile.
I reached down to pick out some cans of soup for myself,
but when I looked back, you were gone.
I stepped from the aisle and saw you at a far corner
checking the date on a carton of eggs.
I hurried toward you.
There were so many things I wanted to say.
About how we took care of Mom
after you were suddenly taken away.
And how our lives turned out rich.
And how we faced life with courage, inspired by you.

As I neared you, a chill touched my cheek.
Soft snowflakes appeared.
Large, fluffy, swirling flakes transfigured
the aisle into an opaque tunnel.
A roiling, white swath accumulated on the tile floor
making it impossible to push the cart.
A final glimpse showed you
walking into the whitened squall.
I reached for you. Called to you.
You disappeared.
The tempest subsided.
I was alone — again.

I paused to breathe,
then moved toward the dairy,
where you stood moments before,
picked up a box of eggs,
and checked its date.

That's when I knew,
I was you.

**What You Do Not Own**

Walk amidst what you do not own:
night, moon, day, sun, soil, water.

Live amidst what you must own:
humility, empathy, compassion.

**Traffic Light**

At the empty intersection,
when all you want is to go straight ahead,
and the red light refuses and refuses
and refuses to change,
it is okay to turn right.

## Embrace Solitude

Embrace the challenge of solitude,
solitude that gives the gift of silence.
Silence which coaxes us to listen,
listen to ourselves in mindful ways.
Ways that lead us to imagine,
imagine about all that brings us passion.
Passion to live in tiny moments,
moments to hold in solemn embrace.

## Cloud

Let me rain on the plants and trees
wetting rocks and sands and seas.
Let me rain on people homeless
and those that suffer loss.
Let me wash away their tears
and cleanse them of their fears.
Let me sprout new life in loam and dirt
growing food for those of broken spirit.
Let me shade the desert from scorching sun
and drop arctic snow as white as cotton spun.
Let me guide those who always falter
and bathe them with my hopeful water.

# Longing

**Butterfly**

As if I were a golden blossom of wallflower,
a monarch landed on my shoulder.
It flitted, circled round and round,
looped and landed on my outstretched palm.

In that instant we were paired,
a regal follow, for my modest lead.
Then together we danced
a waltz, as none else mattered.

Step two-three,
turn two-three,
break two-three,
together two-three,
we bowed two-three and laughed.

When the music stopped it circled,
looped, and landed on my heart,
flapped its wings and left a mark.
An impression that warmed the sun,

and greened the trees,
and stirred the breeze,
and wrote the tunes.
Then it flew away — and lit the moon.

## Table for Two

Subtle diversion in heart of a month
where quiet solitude and promise looms.
Lights softly dimmed, knife touching spoons,
forks gently wrapped in napkins of cloth.

I reach for your hand as memories caress.
Ribboned box filled with sweet divinity.
Heavenly scents of jasmine, pachouli
infuse ivory threads of a wedding dress

hand formed from delicate crewel. First son,
first girl, then three. Nest clears with wee birds' flight.
Promise kept. A lifetime drifts into night.
Your aura is real, not illusion,

sharing this intimate dinner with you,
over a candle lit table for two.

**The Garden**

Winters while I work, you sleep.
Resting through frigid air,
wind and clouds,
and snow.
You replenish.
You refresh.
Do I miss you?
Yes.

When spring sun beckons,
you awaken at the ready.
You call. I answer.
I plant.
So caring.
So gentle.
Did you miss me?
Yes?

She's sleeping, never to return.
Ash to dust to dirt.
She guides my hand.
We tend.
She through me.
Me to you.
Do you miss her?
Too?

## The Button

My trousers lost a button today.
A reminder that when you were here
you could reattach it in minutes,
and life would always go on as before.

I'm not skilled at threading needles
since my fingers are no longer nimble nor adept.
Only on rare occasions am I able to accomplish
this task on the first attempt.

I don't know if the stitching should go crisscross,
horizontal or perhaps with the vertical.
My stitches don't match the holes,
leaving backings that are far from symmetric.

I struggle to push the needle through the fabric,
causing me to poke my finger at least once.
The thread knots as I pull it through,
forcing a restart of the process.

When finished, the button, never in its original position,
will forever awkwardly slip through the hole,
stressing my inadequacies and reinforcing
that life will never go on as before.

**Embers**

Red hot wood crackles
in the fire pit beneath
a half-moon's light.
Scents of honeysuckle

sprinkle the air. Our friends have
gone — their separate ways.
No more talk, or laughter.
Holding a skewered

marshmallow over burning
coals, I am aware of
your presence in the
wispy shimmering glow.

## After the Rain

Storm on my right.
Sun to my left.
I sit between,
among birds, trees,
and river. I
draw in fragrant
rain-cooled air and
think of how much
you loved quiet,
pensive evenings.

**At the Feeder**

Against a dense graphite sky,
a pair of finches dine at the feeder.
Grumbles of thunder join hands
with rips of lightning
behind a wall of roiling scud.

I wonder if finches anticipate storms,
or if they long to dance in the streets,
with heads held back, mouths opened,
and arms raised skyward,
the way we used to do.

Do finches wait until last second
to seek cover? Like the time
we outraced the deluge and
retreated to our room
for an intimate moment
while our children slept.

Could birds be as thrilled
as we were at that angry flash-boom
of cloud-to-ground energy?
The one that had us hugging in laughter,
as deafening waves resonated
through the room before being
replaced by torrents that muffled
our words of commitment.

Perhaps birds share joy in storms.
We did that day. Together.
Lying face to face.
Oblivious to the dictates of the clock.

## Lonely Days

I keep the radio on without listening to what is played,
then write a few lines to fill a mythical quota.
While drinking my morning coffee,
I sit beside my father who died
50 years ago, and read the
newspaper from cover to
cover, the way he always did.
As I walk the dog in daylight,
shadowed night slinks
through fence panels.
The only rhythmic
sound I hear is my
own breathing,
affirming after
all these years,
I can survive
without you.
Like you
said I
could.

**Last Laundry**

I took your final dirty shirt,
and lumped it in with mine.

Next, I placed both in the wash
where the sleeves intertwined
into a knotted fabric ball.
I pulled apart our clinging clothes
and placed them in the dryer.
Where once again they joined,
this time heart to heart.

I took them from the warm machine
and hung mine in the closet.
Then laid yours on our empty bed,
which seemed wider than the sea.

## Of Course She Did

Of course, she'd give her last two coins.
Who wouldn't, when others
needed them so much more?
Losing everything had turned
her world upside down.
But in time, her grief became a friend
who taught that riches
came in forms of people.

She tosses her mite into the basket,
walks to the rear, dissolving
into the shadow of a pillar,
and pleads for strength to travel
this path, which she hadn't chosen.

**Table for Two - II**

Uninvited. Unwanted.
You sit across the table.
I know who you are,
and realize your intentions.

When you first spoke your soothing words
I thought you were trying to help.
"Everything happens for a reason," you said.
Later you took aim at my guilt. My weaknesses.
It didn't take long to know your words
mirrored dark shadows of my inner thoughts.
You stoked my confusions.
Made me question my being.
Over time your intrusions lessened.
For many a dinner you sat in the family room
while I ate my solitary meal.

So now here you are again.
Go ahead. Sit there.
I can tolerate you because I know
most of life is inexplicable.
It's okay. Stay. But on my terms.
Not yours.
Acceptance heals.

**Space Walk**

Do not cast off
the tether that
binds to home.

Therein lies your
inner child.

**Stripped Away**

When life as you know it has been stripped away,
and seems as far off as the ocean,
or the mountains with their
untamed streams and
snow-capped peaks.

And you feel as though you are
in the middle of a field as large
and flat and wide
as Kansas.

When you have no needle or thread
to reattach the button, no pen to sign
your name, or no mark
to hold your place.

And the last time you touched someone,
hugged someone, or kissed someone
was a hundred years ago.

When the whole thing makes you want to
pound the tabletop and scream,
because, what could have been,
what should have been,
is not what is.

That's when Plato's shadows, so flattened
against the wall, step forward,
take shape, and emerge
through the opening
into daylight.

## I Go to Water

I go to water to seek peace.
Water that is still and glass-like.
Glass so finely polished, it mirrors the horizon,
in scene of such beauty, that it begs me to
take its picture.

I go to water to seek humility.
Water that is white-capped with
frothing waves, as winds push it
against itself. Waves that crash with
a force I cannot possibly match.

I go to water to talk.
Water that gurgles in its meandering,
downward path to the sea.
Meandering waters that listen unconditionally,
with neither interruption nor judgement.

I go to water to breathe.
Water that cleanses the air with scents of moss
and silt and damp grasses.
Bouquets that coax my inner child
to create with passion and energy.

I go to water to wander.
Water that stirs my imagination,
to wander into worlds I have never seen,
museums I wish to explore, and walk beside
long-past ancestors whose genes I carry.

I go to water to wonder.
Water where the blue heron patiently waits,
and stepping stones of blooming lily pads gently bob
along the shoreline. A shore where the quiet folds into itself,
releasing strings that tether my dreams.

When I seek answers, I go to water.

# **Reflecting**

## The Aging Face in the Mirror

And now I know the truth that stares me in the eyes,
a life of love and loss, and age with compromise.
Winter's harshest winds have nothing to compare,
to the sting of furrowed skin, and thinning, graying hair.
The facts reflected in my face, through wrinkles and fine lines,
are life's major turning points, that every etch defines.

A crease atop the forehead, marks victory o're disease.
Several lines below are from mourning loves deceased.
Beside the eyes lie crow's feet, fanning out for all to see,
exposing random wins and losses, that life's tossed out to me.
At lips, the smile, that once was proud and ever ready,
is now a drooping frown, that renders me unsteady.

The image tells a story, a truth I can't deny,
this life is short and fragile. I daren't live for days gone-by.
It shows this person, who once was young, and taut, and strong,
may be no longer bound to walk this Earth for very long.
But the vision that sends me back, also brings me to the 'fore,
confirming change, life's only way, to gift me even more.

## Reflections

Light of Crescent Moon reflects off glass-like water,
inviting inner peace. Venus, a vivid evening star,
stands beside in confirmation. Welcome
the call to breath rhythmically,
slow thoughts, calm
emotions, sense
being. Inhale
the fragrance
of dusk.

**Naked**

As babes, we come into the world,
untouched, unspoiled, dancing free,
singing loud with outstretched arms.
Hearts open to the stars,
we stroll through unlatched doors,
seeking playful comfort,
in an unvarnished universe.

Soon we see our imperfections,
an initial loss of our virginity.
And now we plead, just accept me as I am,
when I know you and you know me.

Thrust into a world of ambiguity,
the search for open truth becomes
a base for affirmation.
Our gentle tears rain down
as we walk Mother Earth,
surviving to now from naked birth.

## The Visitor

My reflection
stares back though
the living room glass.
I am alone. I am cold.
Rain falls heavy in
wind-driven, diagonal sheets.
Ripples race across ponding flows.
Rivulets join to streams to rivers to seas.
A robin hunts for worms.
Fallen needles cover ground beneath a pine.
Wilted wildflowers lie in state along a forsaken path.
Crocuses inch upward then droop from lack of water.
The creek-bed is dry and lifeless,
and the soil is caked, not fertile.
Desert sands blow skyward
in rising clouds of dust.
A baby cries.
A stray dog howls.
A mother has no money for food.
The sun sets in a colorless sky,
as unsettled thoughts linger,
like the visitor who won't leave.

**Dark Matter**

Unseen particles amass
between spectral
specks of starlight.

Unspoken thoughts
lie veiled behind
the conscious mind.

Waves of light
made brilliant by a blackened
space-time curtain.

True self visible
through shadowed lens
of prior silent sorrow.

Light and life,
ambiguous spectra of
seeable and unseeable,

opened and secret,
spoken and silent,
reachable and unreachable.

An essential paradox.
Know darkness.
Know brilliance.

**Morning Walk in the Country**

I step from the roadside
and stop beside barbed wire
to gaze at giant rounds of hay
resting in a rolling field.

The morning air is filled
with scents of newly
mown grasses, already
vowing to regrow.

Beside a drowsy house
and barn, a windmill's
stationary blades await
the first puff of wind.

Overhead a hawk circles
in search of breakfast,
as its reflection floats
swan-like over a pond.

The walk continues, and
I wonder how untroubled
life would be if my mind
were this serene.

**Walk a Paved Path**

Walk a paved path, where many others have traveled,
so as not to waste a surface drawn from deep earth.

It has been laid down by calloused hands. Smoothed by strong
people, so you may move with ease. Though it covers

a worn, dirt trail, wisdom of the sentinel oak
reminds us that it is part of the wild forest.

And like the tree, it has sprung from soil, and water,
and air. Different. Not different. But part of.

### Sun Rose in the Eastern Sky

Sun rose in the Eastern sky
bathing all in coral hues.
Daffodils bloom.
Chickadees sing.
Dog's tail wags.

Sun sets in the Western sky
painting all in golden tones.
While Spring's waning moon awaits
to bestow its crescent call:
breathe, reflect, let go.

**Conversations with Crescent Moon**

"You look troubled,"
Crescent Moon said to me.
"Yes. I'm worried, tired, and need to go to bed,"
I answered, as I rose from my chair by the garden.
"Please. Stay," Crescent Moon urged. "I can help.
Let me bathe you in scents of blooming hyacinth
to ease your trouble mind. I will conduct for you
a symphony of chirping crickets backed
by rhythmic calls of distant killdeer.
With this, I will lullaby you to sleep. To peace. To harmony."
I returned to my seat, and Crescent Moon
wrapped me in the serenity of dusk.

## Conversations with Crescent Moon - II

"You are worried, I can see it in your gait,"
Crescent Moon said, as I walked a wooded path
beneath his quiet light.
"Yes. I am troubled by these days.
I always figured a time would come,
that I'd have to put things in a vessel
to remind the world that I was here.
Now, I'm afraid I have to act."
I spoke while walking past the old oak
and side-stepping a sleeping wildflower.
"That vessel is for others," said Crescent Moon.
"The things you speak of, are your story.
A tale of your life, who you are, and what you were.
Think less about what you include,
and more about what you exclude."
As I continued my walk, I noticed the
delicious fragrance of still, night air.

## Somewhere

Somewhere between infinity and the atom,
there is being.
>   You. Me. All.

Somewhere between lullaby and requiem,
we question.
>   Who? What? Why?

Somewhere between pilgrimage and homage,
we struggle.
>   Grief. Denial. Regret.

Somewhere between Winter and Summer,
comes Spring.
>   Emerge. Breathe. Blossom.

Somewhere between hearing and listening,
we tell stories.
>   Yours. Mine. Everyone's.

Somewhere between cause and effect,
we find empathy.
>   Injure. Apologize. Forgive.

Somewhere between darkness and day,
dawns a new somewhere.
>   For you. For me. For all.

## The Painted Corner

Breathing slows as we recover
from our privacy. Bent knees touch
like nesting spoons.

You turn to face me and our lips
meet in quiet oneness. Soft whispers
exchange intimate thoughts.

You brush a bead of dew
from my forehead, then shiver
as I press a finger to your lips.

I start to put an arm around you,
then hesitate like a widow
pausing at the grave.

I try to meet your gaze
but you look past me,
as if searching for a truth
in the painted corner of the room.

Though we are as close
as two can be,
we are oceans apart.

## She Boards the Last Train Out of Town

She boards the last train out of town
uncaring about its destination.
The steam engine puffs
black smoke as it groans
forward in slow motion.
The car in which she sits
begrudgingly follows
as it leaves the station.
A tear trickles down her cheek
as she looks out the window
to the platform and spies her heart
resting on a satchel of broken promises.

## Intersection

Dust swirls skyward
in dry summer
winds, as Jack pines
bow side to side.

Hot, thirsty, and
tired of walking.
Wonder which dirt
road leads me home?

## At the Freeway Entrance

She looked into the rearview mirror
for a last glance at her home.
No — a last glance at her soul.

The horizon glowed orange
as long spires of clouds rose skyward.
Had she turned off the lights?
And the coffee pot?
Did it matter? Did she care?

Would anything in her life
matter to that homeless man
in the park who clung tightly to
his few possessions locked
in a discarded Amazon box?
She could be he in another hour,
another day, or another week.

Would it matter to the little girl inside
wanting only to dance in sunlight?
Would it matter to her aging self
desiring nothing more
than to share her wisdom?

She needed change.
"Go east," they said.
East meant family, friends, and comfort.
East promised a safe life,
with safe dreams and safe hopes.

She looked back and held out an opened hand,
as if holding the past in her palm.
Then blew a goodbye kiss, after which
she paused, smiled,
and drove west.

**Push, Pull**

Push, Pull
forces we
control

Open, Close
mindsets we
impose

Grasp, Release
choosing brings
us peace

## The Mirror

I am nothing more than fired sand,
soda ash, and limestone. One side
coated with silver and the other polished smooth.

Dare to imagine, that you step through my surface
into a world where Tweedle Dee and Tweedle Dum
teach you to run before you walk.

A land where Alice offers new perspectives,
and second chances to right wrongs.
Chances to love the face you see.

I reflect you. But this view
is one where right is left and left is right.
Walk forward, touch and study what you see.

Your face. A wonderful face,
in which every wrinkle sings a song,
and every line weaves a tale.

Every time you look at me, you see a different person.
A new reference with no questions or judgments.
Those can only come from you. Say your name.

Say it again. And again. Let me help you
know what's inside. For you cannot know the image,
if you do not know yourself.

## A Soft Snow

A soft snow fell upon a field
of dried, browned goldenrod,
concealing secrets below.

A pine standing sentry at field's edge,
collected the snow on its branches,
cradling it safely in its grip.

Though the sun tried, it could not,
or would not pierce the overcast.
A calm silence reigned, as boughs
drooped under the weight of white.

## Moon

Moon, I see you standing all alone,
a soft sliver in a starless gulf,
your crescent tips pointing
to where Orion once sheathed his sword.
No twinkling specks of light,
no Leo, Virgo, or Hercules
to usher you along.
Where are the gods, Mercury,
Jupiter, and Mars? And where is Venus?

What did you do to deserve such fate?
Arrantly snatch fire from the sun?
Darken van Gogh's Starry Night?
Or are you simply weary
from your nightly heavens climb?

Slowly, lonely, you wander blackened sky.
Gaze upon Earth. Breathe in the rich perfume
of spring honeysuckle. See me,
seeing you, through the flickering glow
of a thousand fireflies.
Hold my gaze and speak to me.
I will listen to your story.
I will write your poems.
I will join you, and together
we will navigate the void.

## The Climb

Another year alone,
another restart toward
the summit.
Footstep follows footstep,
exhausted breath
follows exhausted breath.

I keep looking forward,
because looking back
means knowing how far
I've come, and how steep
the climb has been.

# Emerging

## The Owl and the Lark

Dawn arrives as daylight breaks,
the Owl stirs, the Lark awakes.

Divergent birds bid day anew,
in cover kissed by morning dew.

On single oak with diff'rent clock,
as though opposing sides of block.

The Lark flits about its day,
the Owl perched, not yet to prey.

By tree they're joined in union dance,
present by choice, not happenstance.

Each bird fulfills through gives and takes,
that which for both, life better makes.

Unlikely paired as two shall be,
yet each maintains own dignity.

Daylight fades with evening sun.
Owl renews. Lark's work is done.

## The Perseids

Meteor.
Falling star.
Remnant of comet.
Born through Perseus,
to a momentary flare of life.
Do you know the ways you inspire?
Are you aware of the beauty of your brilliance?
Can you sense the joy in all who glimpse your fiery path?
Your fleeting existence within the cosmic vastness lends hope.

Beholder.
Curious one.
Born from Woman.
Descendent of Earth,
to an instant in geologic time.
Do you know the ways you inspire?
Are you aware of the beauty of your brilliance?
Can you sense the joy in all who follow your spirited path?
Your fleeting existence within the cosmic vastness lends hope.

We
    Are
        Perseids.
           Star
              Dust.
                Awaken.
                  Live.
                    L
                      o
                        v
                          e
                            .

## She Danced on White Sand Dunes

She danced on white sand dunes
beside warm, green water,
her long hair streaming
with each glorious step,
while swaying and circling
in eve's golden light.

She danced and danced.
No person could stop her.
She'd crushed barriers
that stemmed the tides of joy.
A joy which poured in
from all directions.

She gazed the wine-hued sunset
with eyes of blue, blue as the
flowing silk-like dress she wore.
A dress she donned to celebrate
her new-found freedom
from the bondage of hidden lies.

She walked to the water,
and waded along the shoreline
of uncertainty. The sea retreated,
and returned with a gentle breaking wave
that washed all doubts away.

In the darkening dusk
she reached skyward
and pinned her heart
to the crescent moon
for all to see.

**Painting with Oils**

In a world where lies bring darkness,
only truth could give her light.

So she dipped a brush in daytime,
and painted the nighttime bright.

An artist who spent her life
in a sea of white and black.

She smiled at her canvas,
walked away didn't look back.

**Star Fall**

Do you remember that falling star
above the river so wide,
as it whisked silently over the Pleiades?

Do you remember the thrill we had
when we pointed and cheered its appearance,
so anticipated yet fleeting?

Do you remember how our hearts beat as one
at the moment we hugged in celebration,
of that celestial sighting?

Yes. That one moment by the river.
In the darkness, beneath the Milky Way dome.
That's the thrill I get when you smile as we dance.

## Moonlit Snow

freshly fallen snow
under cloudless midnight sky
full moon lustrously
glimmers reflections of soft
moon shadow kisses

**I Step Toward You**

Amidst the luminous
light of a hundred fireflies,
beneath smiling Crescent Moon,
I step toward you,
slowly, cautiously,
with heart in hand.

**It's Okay**

"It's okay,"
her spirit whispered in my ear.
"Your happiness and joy
are what holds me near.
Your love of life
and tender heart,
all I held so dear,
must pass to another,
for you to persevere."

## Honey Bee

You are not a honey bee,
nor are you a daffodil.
You are not a butterfly,
nor are you a chickadee.

You are the tranquil sea.
You are the rising moon.
You are the falling star.
You are — infinity.

## The Cotton Mask

Your cute cotton mask, adorned
with many country roosters,
cannot hide the smile
that reveals your thoughts
about what I mean to you
as we venture on our path.

**Split Personality**

So many times, I feel half hero
and half child lost in the forest.
You make me forget the second part.

**Sky as Clear as Sky Can Be**

A day as bright as day is long,
with sky as clear as sky can be.
No dazzling sun has ever shone,
so brilliant, as the smile you smile at me.

**Triangulation**

I love it when you text
a picture of the moon to me.
Right after I've texted
a picture of the moon to you.
Though miles apart, it feels
as if we're standing side-by-side.

## She Swam in Moonglade

He loved her in the darkness,
and at the break of dawn.
He loved her at the height of noon,
and at dusk when day had waned.
He loved her in fluorescent light,
with bright tones and hues of gold.
He loved her in the Winter,
in the Summer, Spring, and Fall.
But when she swam in moonglade,
he loved her most of all.

## I Know a Place

I know a place on Saturn,
you can't see it but it's there.
A place that we can walk to,
then climb a staircase to the edge.
Where we can leap onto the rings,
and dance to music of the spheres.
We'll sway among the remnants
of cosmic dust and stones,
that light the night in vivid shades
of reds and yellows and golds.

With my lead, and with your follow,
we will step from ring to ring.
Then leap onto a comet's tail,
a fitting floor of glowing ice.
One hand in hand, one hand on shoulder,
we'll turn with rhythmic flair
as the celestial orb transports us
along its distant solar path.

I know a place on Saturn,
you can't see it but it's there.
A place where we can hug
beneath a billion specks of stars.
You'll place your hands upon my cheeks,
I'll run my fingers through your hair.
We'll kiss beneath the great moon, Titan,
bathing in its golden hue,
while whispering words of tenderness,
that only we will hear.

I know a place on Saturn,
you can't see it but it's there.
Take my hand and run with me
to a spot that's ours and ours alone.
For in that place on Saturn's rings,
we are stardust, ever dancing, ever paired.

# About the Author

Peter Donndelinger turned to writing after retiring from a forty-year career as a science and chemistry teacher. In this time, he has penned numerous poems, short stories, and a yet to be published novel.

Peter is active with several southwest Wisconsin writing groups. He can often be spotted writing in local coffee shops, or reading at open mics. Other interests include bicycling, ballroom dancing, photography, and walking Elie, his Golden Retriever.

More of Peter's work can be found in *Bramble Literary Magazine* (Summer 2020) and *Lost and Found: Tales of Things Gone Missing*.

Made in the USA
Monee, IL
17 December 2021

85998152R00049